Philosopher Dog®

LUNCH WITH DIOGENES
The Greek Philosopher and The Philosopher Dog

Dedicated to Art Buchwald,

our favorite philosopher

All of the quotations beneath the photographs

in this book have been attributed to the Greek

philosopher Diogenes of Sinope

in the 4th century BC.

"Dogs and Philosophers do the greatest good
and get the fewest rewards."

This is an intertwined tale of the wise sayings of the Greek philosopher Diogenes of Sinope (who lived like a dog), illustrated by photographs of a rescue dog named Diogenes (who has a touch of the philosopher), and the parallels between them that lead us to discover ancient truths, more relevant than ever for our lives today.

All of the quotations beneath the photographs in this book have been attributed to the philosopher Diogenes, who lived more than 2,000 years ago and believed that the only way to learn a philosophy is by seeing a philosopher in action. Or in this tale, just by watching our Philosopher Dog.

DieAwGinKnees@gmail.com   www.PhilosopherDog.com

This book would not have been possible without Bartlett Russell and John Bergin, whose sweat equity merits our highest gratitude. Without their stalwart support, neither dog nor authors would have survived, literally or figuratively, the ordeals of authorship. Nora Jean Levin and Sandra and Jim Herbert believed in this book from the start. Louise Farmer Smith, a writer par excellence, gave unstintingly of her time and expertise to our endeavor. Thank you!

Praise came from around the world:

From Beirut, Lebanon, Paul Saleh wrote: **"In today's hyperactive, convoluted world, this story is simple, clear, funny, and truthful."** From Brighton, England, Elisabeth Millar expressed: **"A wise, inspiring, and timeless book that transcends generations."**

From New York City, Cintra Wilson mused: **"I got a sustained LOL at my favorite page where the dog is wearing an entire Oompa Loompa suit."** In Washington, DC, Donna Burnett added: **"This little book is amazing in how uplifting it is! It made me laugh out of pure joy"**; and Jim Oliver admitted: **"I don't like dogs, but if I did, I'd buy this book."**

From Arusha, Tanzania, Pat Williamson believes: **"A look from this dog opens the way to your very soul. Don't turn away. He has a message we should all be listening to."**

To name all who cheered this book is nigh to impossible. So thank you! The whole lot of you.

Diogenes of Sinope was a famous Greek philosopher in the 4th century BC who would introduce himself by saying:

"I am Diogenes the dog."

Believing that the only way to teach a philosophy was by showing a philosopher in action, he lived on the streets, kindred to all dogs.

The original performance philosopher, Diogenes taught by example and was sought out as a teacher by the most powerful men of his day, including Alexander the Great.

Throughout time, the identifying symbol of this enlightened philosopher has been a shining lantern. He was recognized throughout Athens and much of the ancient world as the one who wandered in broad daylight, waving a bright lantern, and crying aloud:

"I am searching for an honest man!"

Diogenes the Greek philosopher died in 323 BC.
Above, he carries his lantern alongside a faithful dog.

Diogenes the dog is part Chihuahua, part Akita—a Chikita. Also a little bit Bulldog, he has the heart of a philosopher.

A rescue mutt, he and his starving mother were chained to an abandoned trailer. So flea-bitten, he was literally hairless when found. He quickly developed the skills needed for survival and seems to have forgiven, if not forgotten, whatever sins were visited on him as a puppy. Now, he thrives as a "no harm, no foul" playfellow for dogs and humans alike.

He and I lunch together in "Doggie Park" because of a promise to my married son and his wife "to take this pup for a few walks," just now and then, when they absolutely can not take time from their busy professional lives.

I had hoped to become a grandmother, but instead, I am stuck with a Chikita named Diogenes. So I put the best of all spins on it: The dog needs a walk. I can use the exercise. The dog's hungry, and I have to eat. A professional photographer, I pack a camera in our lunchbox, just in case.

And so begins lunch with Diogenes.

**Diogenes the Philosopher Dog was born in AD 2007.
He wears his lantern as a collar.**

"Of what use is a philosopher who doesn't hurt anyone's feelings?"

CONTENTS

A percentage of all proceeds goes to animal rescue shelters worldwide.

A Dog

I dutifully pick him up on my first day's lunch break. He greets me with a gift, a toy, trying to muster two in his tiny jaws, as if to say, "Here, lady person. We can't have you toyless. Take this ball." I laugh as he wiggles, licks, and nuzzles me with great expectancy.

Given what I know of where this mutt was rescued—chained with his starving mother to an old abandoned trailer—it's clear that he's developed a few survival skills: Share your toys, and develop a winning personality ASAP. So, having won me over as his latest existential challenge, off we go to our neighborhood market to buy the lunch specials.

It takes all of two blocks for me to realize that I have signed up for more than lunch. People begin to smile at us and laugh at his puppy antics as we mosey down the street. A woman leans over to pet him and beams back at me:

"Oh my heavens! He is adorable. He's so cute. What's his name?"

Uh oh. Deep breath.

I think maybe I can say "Rover" and get away with it, but I see the puppy looking up at me as if to say, "Now, be honest."

**"I am Diogenes the Dog.
I nuzzle the kind, bark at the greedy, and bite scoundrels."**

"Diogenes," I sheepishly reply.

She bolts upright. "What's Da Gyno's Disease?"

"No, no, it's Diogenes. *Die-Aw-Gin-Knees*. My son and his wife named him that. He's not my dog. I'm just the GranDogMa. Nothing much to do with him...really," I offer, maybe a bit too emphatically.

She looks at me skeptically. I might as well have been saying the dog's running for President.

"*Die-Aw-Gin-Knees*," she repeats phonetically. "Hmm. What's that mean?"

"Oh, um...well, it's...complicated."

She resolutely backs away from us, muttering, "Uh huh...well, I declare."

At this moment, I realize that I have absolutely no idea what, or who, this *"Die-Aw-Gin-Knees"* really is.

"No one can live with me; it would be too inconvenient."

Later, having bought our lunch, I sit in Doggie Park with my half of the sandwich. I watch Diogenes as he begins to figure out the world.

"This is good to eat; this is better; this is no good at all. Yuk."

I notice small lessons that he's taking from—and offering back to—the little world he's coming to know: "Watch. Pay attention. Be careful of those you invite into your life. Smell first. Little is ever lost; keep on exploring. If the stick's too big to carry, well…just pee on it and let it go. The world will know you were here. But don't forget to come back and pee on it again...just to be sure."

Compared to the utterly forgettable hassles that seem to consume most of us on a daily basis, Diogenes seems to focus on the present, with an honest urgency toward simplicity. It's almost as if the dog's instinctively demonstrating a way of living that focuses on the really important things. As kids and grown-ups pass by, each connected to some type of electronic device, they barely engage with one another or notice there's a cool breeze, or dancing sunlight, or even an interesting stick. It begins to dawn on me that the way I've been doing things may be totally arbitrary and not at all the best way to live.

Is it my imagination, or is this dog almost becoming philosophical, teaching *me* by example? I definitely need to look into this Diogenes fellow.

When asked how one could become famous, Diogenes replied:
"By worrying as little as possible about fame."

"Give an honest bark at the truth."

"I peed on the man who called me a dog.
Why was he so surprised?"

"We can only explain you, young man,
by assuming your father was drunk the night he begot you."

"If you've turned yourself out so handsomely, young man,
if for men, it's unfortunate; if for women, it's unfair."

"It is better to have one friend of great value
than many friends who are good for nothing."

**"The contest that should be for truth and virtue
is for sway and belongings instead."**

"Dogs live in the present with no anxiety.
They know who is friend and who is foe."

"A friend is one soul abiding in two bodies."

"We have two ears and one tongue
so that we would listen more and talk less."

**Alexander the Great offered to grant the Philosopher any request.
Diogenes replied: "Stand less between the sun and me."**

A Philosopher

Unexpectedly, every lunch shared with Diogenes now includes reading all I can about his namesake. And I pack a camera in our lunchbox too, so that I can see with steadfast attention if this foundling mutt is showing me something I need to learn.

In my research I soon discover that the first Diogenes was a Greek philosopher, from Sinope (a province in northern Greece), who lived more than 2,000 years ago in Athens. He died in Corinth at the age of 90 in 323 BC. That same year, his most famous admirer, Alexander the Great, died at age 33.

Diogenes was a man so committed to fundamental and simple truths that he literally lived like a dog to demonstrate his disdain for the materialism and hypocrisy he saw in the world. He wanted to show true honesty, the vital over the irrelevant, and the values he deemed essential for living a meaningful life.

He was, for example, the first person to state, "I am a citizen of the world" (*kosmopolites* in Greek, or cosmopolitan) and was one of the first to suggest that anyone, no matter their social position, was entitled to say what they wanted.

Kindred to all dogs, this Greek philosopher did everything in public. His home was a

**When asked what he could do, Diogenes replied:
"Govern men."**

barrel; his clothes were discards; yet he respected his own feelings, needs, and instincts. He remained loyal to his friends, protecting them and goading them onto the right path.

He literally barked at the truth and growled at lies or what we today would call "Orwellian doublespeak." Furthermore, he warned that we must strive for moral self-mastery and right reason or we'd be ruled by the halter of tyranny. "Reason or a halter"; it's our only choice.

Hmm, could the photos I'm eagerly composing of my lunch companion evoke such wisdom—doglike or otherwise? As I gaze at the pictures I've taken of this ragamuffin, I wonder if this ancient philosopher's spirit might still be residing in a little dog's demeanor?

I am amazed to learn that in Greek, the word for dog is *kyon*, and doglike is *kynikos*, which, through something of a regrettable historical hiccup, evolved into a pejorative, meaning cynic and cynical.

So, one of the first Canine or Cynic Philosophers was Diogenes. How cynicism came to be associated with pessimism, undue skepticism, or lack of faith is lost to history, but it would certainly surprise the original Diogenes, who not only died an optimist, but also believed that we can still help one another become better people.

Alexander the Great said:
"If I were not Alexander, I should wish to be Diogenes."

Then I came across an article in *The New York Times,* "Cynicism We Can Believe In," by Simon Critchley, that pointed out to me just how immediate the value of Diogenes' *kynikos* and his symbolic lantern are to our lives today:

"In a world like ours, which is slowly trying to rouse itself from the dogmatic slumbers of boundless self-interest, corruption, lazy cronyism, and greed, it is Diogenes' lamp that we need to light our path."

"We have complicated every simple gift of the gods."

"Plato's philosophy is an endless conversation."

"There is no society without law;
no civilization without a city."

**"It was a favorite expression of Theophrastus
that time was the most valuable thing a man could spend."**

The Philosopher Diogenes asked Alexander the Great what his plans were.

Alexander the Great answered that he planned to conquer and subjugate Greece.

"Then what?" asked Diogenes.

He planned to conquer and subjugate Asia Minor.

"And then?"

Alexander planned to conquer and subjugate the world.

"What next?"

After all that conquering and subjugating, Alexander the Great planned to relax and enjoy himself.

Diogenes responded:

"Why not save yourself a lot of trouble by relaxing and enjoying yourself now?"

"I have seen the victor Dioxippus subdue all at Olympia
and be thrown on his back by the glance of a girl."

When asked whether it's better to marry or not, Diogenes replied:
"Whatever you do, you will repent it."

"Reason or a halter."

"Aristotle has to dine when Philip of Macedonia
thinks fit; Diogenes can dine at any time he chooses."

**When asked what was the most beautiful thing in the world,
Diogenes replied: "Freedom of Speech."**

Diogenes wandered throughout Athens in broad daylight, waving a lantern and shouting aloud: "I am searching for an honest man."

"I know nothing except the fact of my own ignorance."

A Philosophy for Our Times

Over the course of the following weeks, I read more on Diogenes the Philosopher, while avidly photographing Diogenes the Dog. I discovered even more parallels with my lunch companion and his renowned namesake, both of whom seemed to intuit that your material circumstances have little to do with real happiness.

The philosopher believed that only by striving for integrity, honesty, and responsibility in our life can we attain some measure of deep satisfaction and sustained happiness.

In any difficult situation, we want to point the finger at the perpetrators of injustice, at the corruption of power, at the extortion of the weak, and at the blatant hypocrisy of those entrusted with governance.

As much as we'd like to blame it all on others, would Diogenes point back at us, as well?

After all, much of this is driven by our conspicuous consumption and our conspiracy of the willing to think that we can cheat our way to happiness by ignoring deceit, greed, hypocrisy, and the total betrayal of trust.

"One wrong will not balance another. To be honorable and just
is our only defense against men without honor or justice."

If, according to Diogenes, "He has the most who is content with the least," will living in a larger "barrel" really give us greater contentment?

In Doggie Park, I watch as my Philosopher Dog loses a ball down a storm drain, only to shake it off as something that didn't matter that much. I wonder: Could I lose my own toys so gracefully?

Humans claim to be enlightened, yet we are slaves to our own creations and schedules. We live by markets that we worship as gods; we invest ourselves in toys and houses that don't last; we hang our sense of self on opinion and reputation. Take those from us and we mourn, somehow impoverished, yet still thinking ourselves superior creatures.

But, as Diogenes asks, who is the superior being? The dog who knows it can live without these things, or the man who is afraid he cannot?

If less greed creates more contentment, then perhaps more contentment would allow people to serve with integrity in government, corporate, and moral authorities. With less stuff to clutter our life and our barrel, we might become better stewards of our planet.

Diogenes' symbolic lantern reveals the necessity of becoming "citizens of the world," not in some banal international sense, but in the deeper sense of our interconnectedness with—and interdependence on—one another and nature. After all, we have only one watery blue address: Planet Earth.

Wherever disaster strikes, we sense our global bond by helping those in need. Why can't we retain this bond beyond disasters? Why can't we believe that our common good is the good for all?

The more I delve into this Greek man's life, while trying to illustrate his wise sayings, the more I realize there are truths that are timeless for good reasons, and we forget them at our peril.

"Evil is advanced by the negligence of the good-intentioned and the harmless."

"Pilfering Treasury property is particularly dangerous;
big thieves are ruthless in punishing little thieves."

"To own nothing is the beginning of happiness."

"To be saved from folly
you need either kind friends or fierce enemies."

When dragged off to Macedonia and asked, "Who are you?"
Diogenes replied: "A spy upon your insatiable greed."

When others chided him for being an old man who ought to rest, Diogenes asked: "What if I were running in the stadium...

...ought I to slacken when approaching the goal
but rather shouldn't I put on speed?"

"Man is the most intelligent of the animals...
and the most silly."

"I was once as young and silly as you are now,
but I doubt if you will become as old and wise as I am now."

"He has the most who is content with the least."

Why won't you talk to us, Diogenes? "Because you are too important for my subtlety, and I am too subtle for your importance."

"It is the privilege of the gods to want nothing
and of godlike men to want little."

A Philosopher Dog

On my toughest days, I pick up our Chikita with a little less enthusiasm than I'd like to show. I arrive at the door thin on energy, stretched too far by the many tasks that can drain us all. But within seconds of arriving, I'm pulled out of my self-absorption by some expression on this little mutt's face, which effortlessly leads me to remember why the original Diogenes chose to live like a dog, first, and a philosopher, second:

To remind us that one of our few truly human gifts is that we can recognize ourselves in other animals and, ultimately, be reminded that our dramas, problems, preoccupations, and desires are neither as unique nor as cosmically significant as we often like to believe they are.

We surround our lives with "to do lists," obligations, and technology "time-savers"—what we would call essentials but what the Philosopher Diogenes would call distractions and trivia. He was sought as a teacher, in part, because he decried these menial time sinks of everyday life as impostors.

Remembering this helps whenever I feel like I'm being overwhelmed by our techno-savvy existence and start to take life a bit too seriously. "Live life well, not ill" is one of Diogenes' many aphorisms that I find myself quoting, smiling at the dog.

"I am not an Athenian or a Greek;
I am a citizen of the world."

Now, Diogenes and I have lunch together as often as possible (his schedule seems to be filling up).

And, it turns out he likes to have a mission, too.

Wherever I am allowed in with my lunch date, which are more places than I would have anticipated—banks, restaurants, even the Capitol of the United States—something positive begins to happen.

I'm not saying he solves problems himself, only that he helps put problems into context, which, oddly, can sometimes help solve them.

People look up from their desks and smile, forgetting momentarily about some dilemma or wicked problem. They put down phones and leave computers, taking the opportunity to engage with this little guy, who wants nothing from them that they can't offer.

Indeed, it's not long before someone offers him a treat, and it is immediately clear that Diogenes is really, honestly thankful. His gratitude begins to create trust again, like the one I and so many others have lost.

It's as if people see this dog and know, intuitively:

THERE is an honest man.

And sometimes he's free for lunch.

"A friend's hand is always open."

Paris Singer: Co-Author and Photographer
Dr. Adam Russell: Co-Author and Provider of Treats
Bartlett and Adam Russell: Owners of the Philosopher Dog, Diogenes
Photos on pages 9, 55, and 62 are courtesy of Bartlett Anne Russell.

Acknowledgments

Although not one word of Diogenes' sayings survived in written form, his philosophy comes to us through the ages from many sources. We especially acknowledge the modern translations of Diogenes' quotations in Davenport, Guy, *Herakleitos and Diogenes* (Bolinas, CA: Grey Fox Press, 1979).
We thank Ms. Bonnie Jean Cox, Trustee for the Literary Estate of Mr. Guy Davenport, for her kind permissions. Also consulted:
Critchley, Simon, "Cynicism We Can Believe In," *The New York Times,* March 31, 2009.
Hughes, Scott, http://millionsofmouths.com/diogenes.html.
Weir, Anthony, "The Zen of Disengagement: Diogenes of Sinope," at www.beyondthepale.co.uk/diogenes.htm.
Photograph of Diogenes the Greek Philosopher is by the kind permission of Luis E. Navia, author of *Diogenes the Cynic: The War against the World* (Amherst, NY: Humanity Books, 2005).

"I do not know whether there are gods or not,
but there ought to be."

Adam Russell and Paris Singer, mother and son co-authors, live in Washington, DC. They are grateful to Art Buchwald for encouraging their endeavors. Thanks Artie!

Made in the USA
Charleston, SC
18 November 2012